What a Storm!

By Jill Atkins

Published in 2026 by
Norwood House Press
2544 Clinton Street
Buffalo, NY 14224

Printed in the United States of America

Library of Congress Cataloging-in-Publication Data:
Names: Atkins, Jill (Children's author). | Jones, Cath, 1965-, author. | Widdowson, Dan, illustrator.
Title: What a storm / written by Jill Atkins. The long dark trek / written by Cath Jones, illustrated by Dan Widdowson.
Description: Buffalo, NY : Norwood House Press, 2026. | Series: Phonics all-stars: phase 4 |
Identifiers: ISBN 9781978578715 (pbk.) | ISBN 9781978578722 (library bound) | ISBN 9781978578739 (ebook)
Subjects: LCSH: Reading–Phonetic method–Juvenile fiction. | English language–Phonetics–Juvenile fiction. | Storms–Juvenile fiction. | Hiking–Juvenile fiction. | Litter (Trash)–Juvenile fiction. | Environmental responsibility–Juvenile fiction.
Classification: LCC LB1573.3 A796 2026 | DDC 372.465–dc23

CPSIA compliance information: Batch #CW26NHP: For further information contact Norwood House Press at 1-800-237-9932.

When we have a storm, it starts to get dark.

We might need flashlights to see well in the dim light.

There are bright flashes of lightning.

Then we hear a distant growl of thunder.

Soon, the rain lashes down
and the wind howls.

Rain like this might be a monsoon.

There is so much rain!

Some pets do not like storms.

This dog rushes under a bed. Dogs do not like the thunder and the lightning.

This man dashes out of the rain.

This little kid thinks it is fun to get wet.

Do you like to hear thunder? Do you like to see lightning?

It can look stunning as it criss-crosses in patterns.

Lightning can hit a tree.
Then the tree might burn down.

So never shelter under one in a storm.

Some churches have a lightning rod at the top, to keep the lightning off the tower.

In a storm, the air fizzes, lightning flashes and thunder crashes.

What a storm!

In the end, the storm finishes.

The lightning no longer flashes.
The thunder no longer crashes.

The rain stops and it is no longer so dark.

The sun has come out!

The Long, Dark Trek

Written by
Cath Jones

Illustrated by
Dan Widdowson

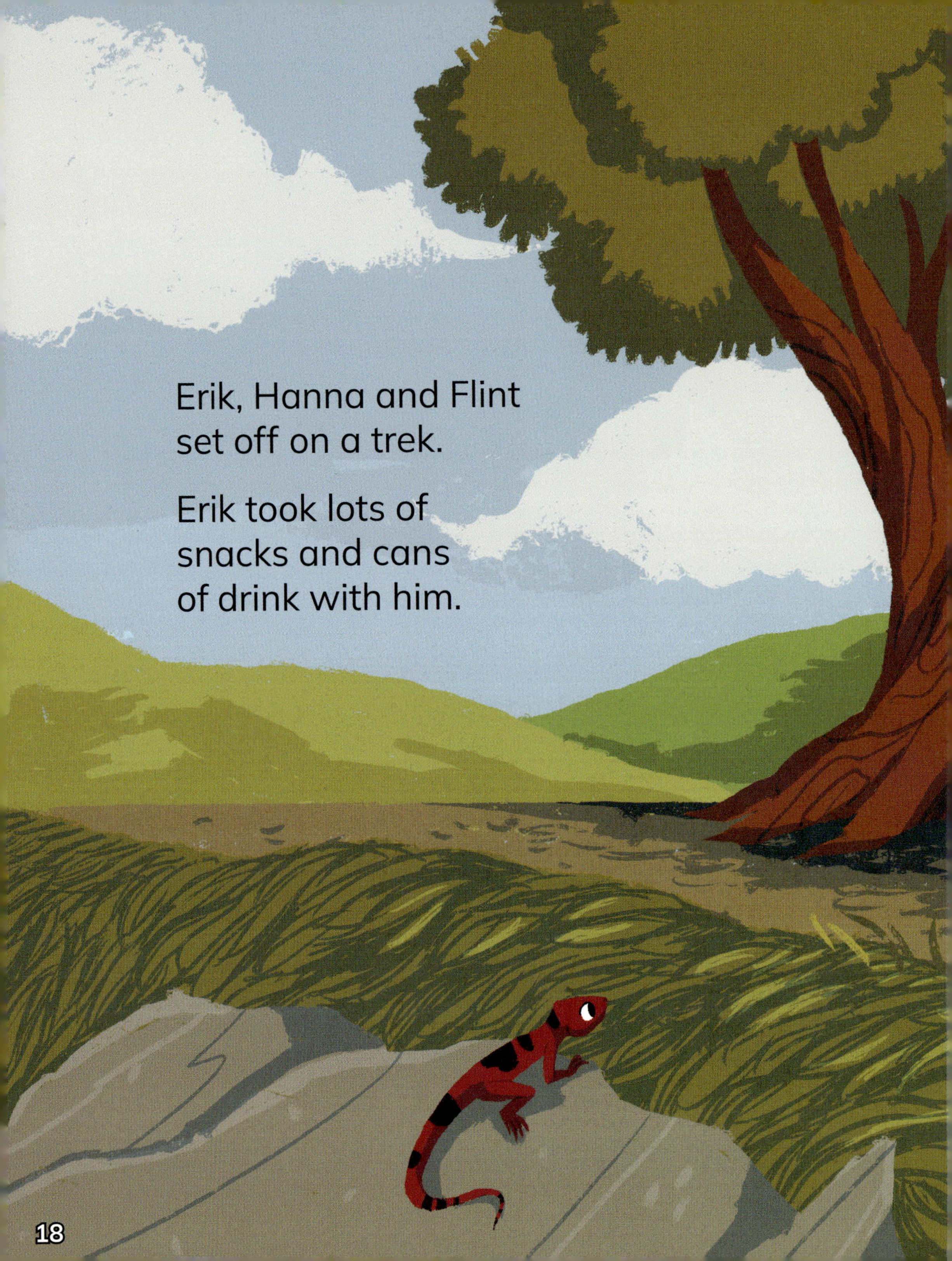

Erik, Hanna and Flint
set off on a trek.

Erik took lots of
snacks and cans
of drink with him.

They went down a long
track and into a wood.

Erik had lots of snacks
as they went.

He left litter on the track and
a drink can on a big tree stump.

A chill wind swept up the track. There was a thick frost on the trees.

"I think we're lost," Hanna said, "and soon it'll be dark!"

They crept down the track.

"We need to get out of this wood," said Flint. "But how?"

“Look!” Erik said. “What’s that?”

It was a gang of litter pickers. They were picking up litter in the wood.

Erik, Hanna and Flint were so glad to see them.

“Greetings!” one of the litter pickers said to them.

“You can help us pick up all this litter. There’s a lot of it on this track – it’s such a mess.”

Erik went a bit red.

“We are so glad to see you,” said Flint. “We’re lost. How do we get out of this wood?”

“Get out?” said the litter picker.
She was looking at the trail
of litter on the track.

"That's no problem at all.

Look, there's a town, right next to the track!"